2ND EDITION

PIANO Adventures® by Nancy and Randall Faber
THE BASIC PIANO METHOD

W9-ALV-015

Thanks and acknowledgment to Victoria McArthur
for her collaboration on the First Edition of this book.

FABER
PIANO ADVENTURES®
3042 Creek Drive
Ann Arbor, Michigan 48108

Write C, G, and F Major Scales

Scale degrees
11/16/16

The major scale has 7 tones called **scale degrees**.
A scale is created from whole steps and half steps.

Review: The half steps are between *scale degrees 3–4* and *degrees 7–8*.
All the other intervals are whole steps.

Example to study:

∨ = half
⌴ = whole

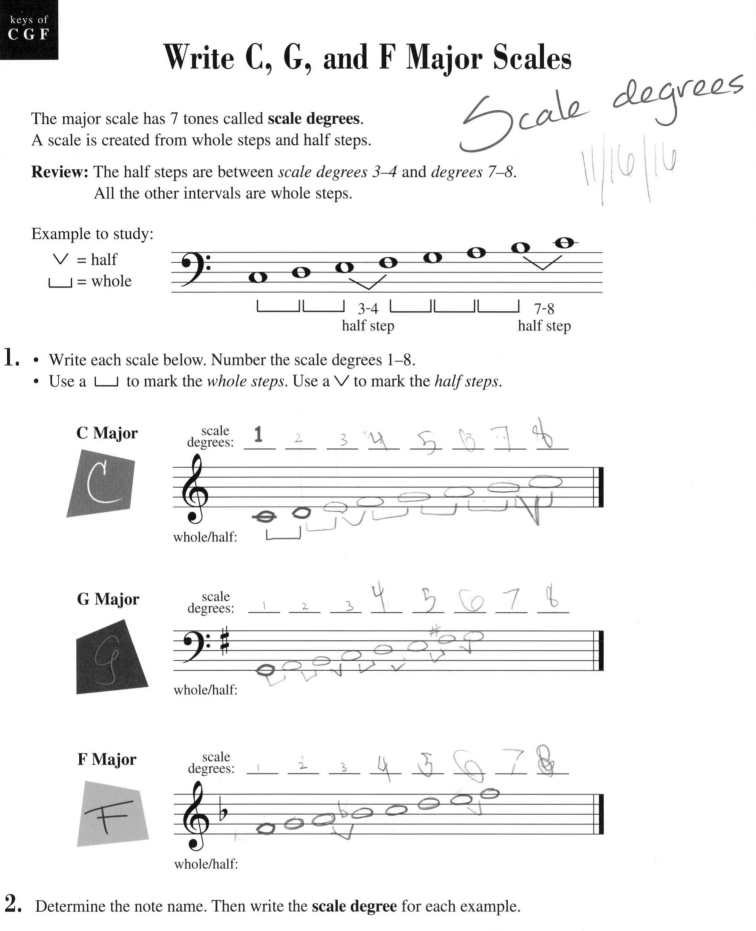

3-4 half step   7-8 half step

1. • Write each scale below. Number the scale degrees 1–8.
   • Use a ⌴ to mark the *whole steps*. Use a ∨ to mark the *half steps*.

C Major

scale degrees: 1 2 3 4 5 6 7 8

whole/half:

G Major

scale degrees: 1 2 3 4 5 6 7 8

whole/half:

F Major

scale degrees: 1 2 3 4 5 6 7 8

whole/half:

2. Determine the note name. Then write the **scale degree** for each example.

Key of C   Key of G   Key of F   Key of F   Key of G

scale degree 5   7   2   4   4

Key Signatures

3. Draw these key signatures for **G major** and **F major**.

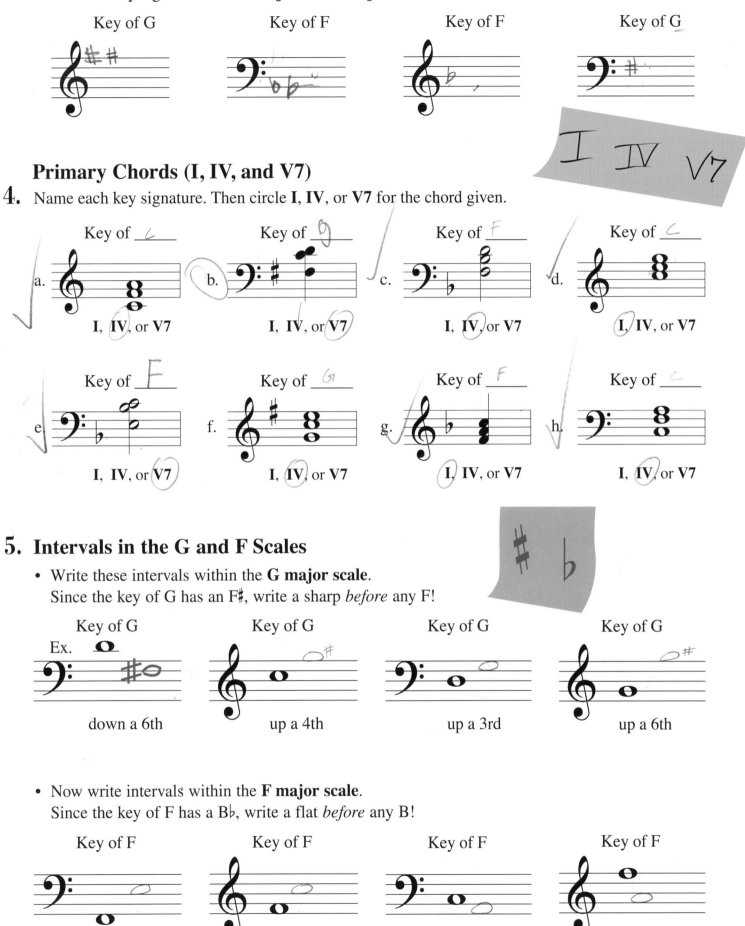

Primary Chords (I, IV, and V7)

4. Name each key signature. Then circle **I**, **IV**, or **V7** for the chord given.

Key of _C_
a.
I, **IV**, or V7

Key of _G_
b.
I, IV, or **V7**

Key of _F_
c.
I, **IV**, or V7

Key of _C_
d.
I, IV, or V7

Key of _F_
e.
I, IV, or **V7**

Key of _G_
f.
I, **IV**, or V7

Key of _F_
g.
I, IV, or V7

Key of _C_
h.
I, **IV**, or V7

5. Intervals in the G and F Scales

- Write these intervals within the **G major scale**.
  Since the key of G has an F#, write a sharp *before* any F!

Key of G
Ex.
down a 6th

Key of G
up a 4th

Key of G
up a 3rd

Key of G
up a 6th

- Now write intervals within the **F major scale**.
  Since the key of F has a Bb, write a flat *before* any B!

Key of F
up a 6th

Key of F
up a 4th

Key of F
down a 2nd

Key of F
down a 5th

The Alberti Bass

The *Alberti bass* is a common L.H. chord pattern.
The chord tones are used in this order: *bottom top middle top*

1. Study these examples. Copy each on the blank staff to the right.

Key of C

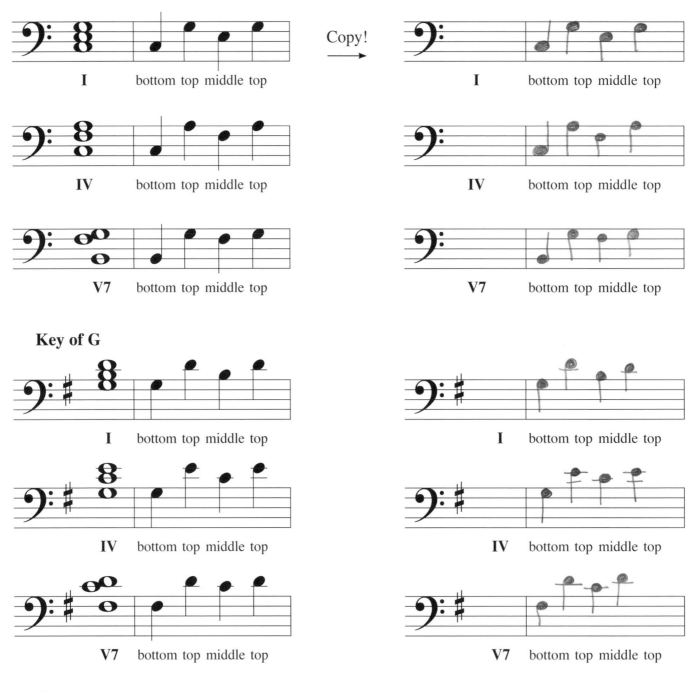

I   bottom top middle top

Copy! →

I   bottom top middle top

IV   bottom top middle top

IV   bottom top middle top

V7   bottom top middle top

V7   bottom top middle top

Key of G

I   bottom top middle top

I   bottom top middle top

IV   bottom top middle top

IV   bottom top middle top

V7   bottom top middle top

V7   bottom top middle top

Close your eyes and *listen*. Your teacher will play example **a** or **b**.
Open your eyes and circle the chord pattern you heard.

Teacher Note: Play in the keys of C, G, or F. Play blocked chords or an Alberti bass!

1a.   **I   V7   I   V7**   2a.   **I   IV   I   V7**   3a.   **I   IV   IV   I**

or   or   or

b.   **I   V7   V7   I**   b.   **I   I   I   IV**   b.   **I   IV   V7   I**

Compose Your Own Sonatina*

2. • Let your ear guide you and compose a R.H. melody over the Alberti bass. A suggested rhythm is shown.

• When you are done, play your sonatina!

A Section

Moderato

_____
(your name)

B Section

D.C. al Fine

3. Circle the correct musical form of this piece:

A B   **A B A**   **A B A B**

*A *sonatina* is an instrumental piece that became especially popular for the piano in the late 1700s.
Many sonatinas use the Alberti bass and usually have more than one movement.

Harmony Rules

We can **harmonize** a melody with **I**, **IV**, and **V7 chords**. Play and *listen* to each example.

Use the **I** chord for scale degrees 1-3-5.

Use the **IV** chord for scale degrees 1-4-6.

Use the **V7** chord for scale degrees 2-4-5.

Key of C: **I**   **IV**   **V7**

1. • Play this ascending C scale. Do you see a rhythm pattern?

   • Harmonize with **I**, **IV**, or **V7** chords. Then play!

Yellow Bird C Scale

• Transpose to **G major**.

2. • Play this descending G scale.

   • Harmonize with **I**, **IV**, or **V7** chords. Then play!

Yellow Bird G Scale

• Transpose to **C major**.

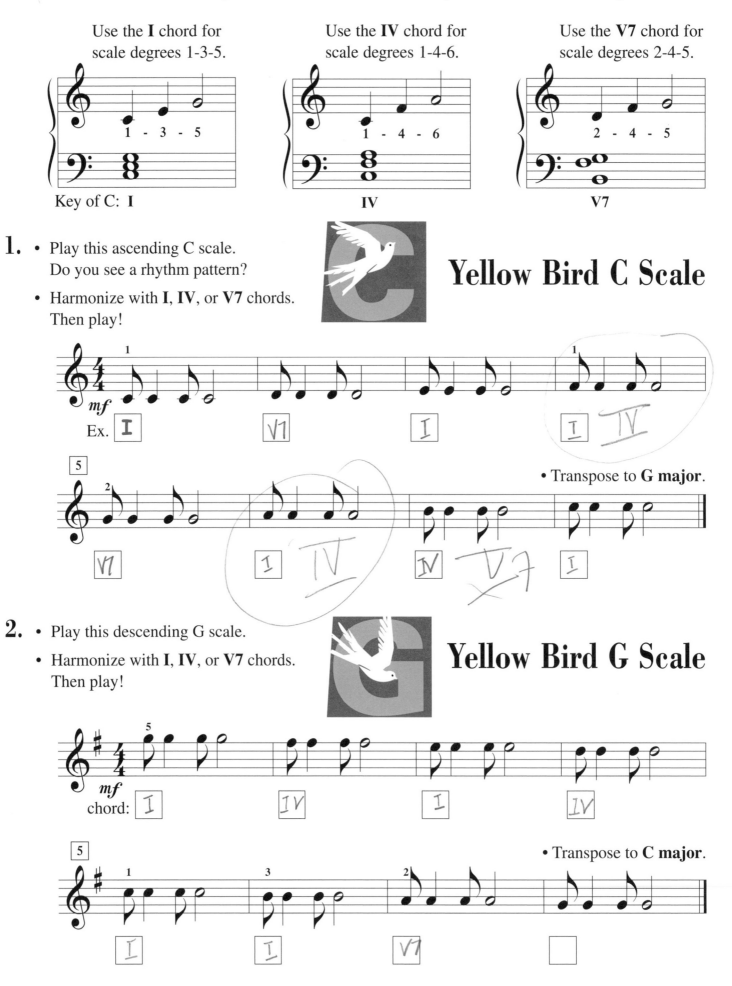

Bar Lines to the Rescue!

Draw **bar lines** for each rhythm. Continue writing in the counts.
Then tap with your teacher. Feel the syncopation!

What's That Chord?

Your teacher will play an Alberti bass pattern
that will end on the **I**, **IV**, or **V7** chord.
Listen and circle the **last** chord you hear.

a.	**I**		b.	**I**		c.	**I**		d.	**I**
	IV			**IV**			**IV**			**IV**
	V7			**V7**			**V7**			**V7**

For Teacher Use Only (The examples may be played in any order and repeated, if needed.)

Lesson pp.14–15 (Yellow Bird)

Theory Pop Quiz

2/1/17

- Explore your theory knowledge!
  Answer these 18 questions about Grieg's piece.

- Now play the piece again. Does it seem easier now?

Morning

Edvard Grieg
(1843-1907, Norway)
arranged

1. Name the **flat** in the key signature. ___Bb___

2. The **8th** notes begin on beat __2__ .

cross over

p

3. Name the **chord**. ___F___

4. Name the **interval**. ___4___

5. Identify the curved line as a **slur** or a **tie**. ___slur___

pedal simile (pedal similarly)

6. Does the L.H. begin on the **tonic** or the **dominant**? ___dominant___

9. Name the **chord**. ___A___

mf

7. Name the **interval**. ___3___

8. Name the **interval**. ___4___

10. Name the two R.H. **accidentals**.
____C#____ and ____B♮____

11. Write the beats **1 2 3** for *measure 20.*

12. Name the **chord tones**.

E top
C# middle
A bottom

13. Name the **chord tones**.

F top
C# middle
A bottom

14. Name the **chord**. ___A___

15. Name the **chord**. ___C___

16. Name the **chord**. ___F___

17. Name the **L.H. ledger note**. ___D___

18. Name the **R.H. interval**. ___6___

Identify and Write Sevenths (7ths)

identify 7ths ✓ 16/17

1. Identify each interval as a **3rd**, **5th**, or **7th**.
   Hint: Count each line and space, including the *first* and *last* note.

a. Ex. __**5th**__

b. __3rd__

c. __7th__

d. __7th__

e. __7th__

f. __5th__

g. __3rd__

h. __7th__

i. __7th__

j. __3rd__

k. __5th__

l. __7th__

write 7ths

2. Write a **7th** up or down from each note. Then name both notes.

a. note names: __G__ __F__
   up a 7th

b. __G__ __A__
   down a 7th

c. __D__ __C__
   up a 7th

d. __G__ __A__
   down a 7th

e. __G__ __F__
   up a 7th

f. __D__ __C__
   up a 7th

Common Time 𝄴 = $\frac{4}{4}$

Cut Time

Cut time, written 𝄵 = $\frac{2}{2}$ beats in a measure
the ♩ gets one beat

Cut time is also known as *alla breve*.

1. This music is in cut time. Write **"1 2"** under the
correct notes to show the beats in each measure.

The Can-Can

Jacques Offenbach
(1819-1880)
arranged

2. Can you transpose *The Can-Can* to **G major**?

Lesson pp.22–23 (Cossack Ride) 11

Sightread these examples.

- Take a moment to scan the music. Watch for **7ths**!
- Set a slow, steady beat for two measures before you begin.

sightread

Your teacher will play either example **a** or **b**. Circle the example you hear.
Your teacher may ask you to play each example on the piano.

Musical Terms

(Review of UNITS 1-2)

2/8/17

1. Write the number of the matching term in each blank.

1. Ostinato   ___3___ the fifth scale degree

2. Tonic   ___11___ two beats to a measure, alla breve

3. Dominant   ___5___ two sections; an A section followed by a B section

4. Leading tone   ___1___ a musical pattern that repeats over and over

5. Binary form   ___8___ a sharp, flat, or natural that is not in the key signature

6. Ternary form   ___7___ a common L.H. chord pattern; bottom-top-middle-top

7. Alberti bass   ___4___ the 7th tone of the scale

8. Accidental   ___2___ the first scale degree

9. Seventh   ___10___ the same as $\frac{4}{4}$

10. Common time   ___6___ three sections; an A section, a B section, and a return to the A section

11. Cut time   ___12___ the distance between two notes on the keyboard or the staff

12. Interval   ___9___ one note smaller than an octave

2. Create a keyboard example of each of these for your teacher.

seventh   Alberti bass   ostinato

2/22/17

Rhythm Talk in $\frac{3}{8}$

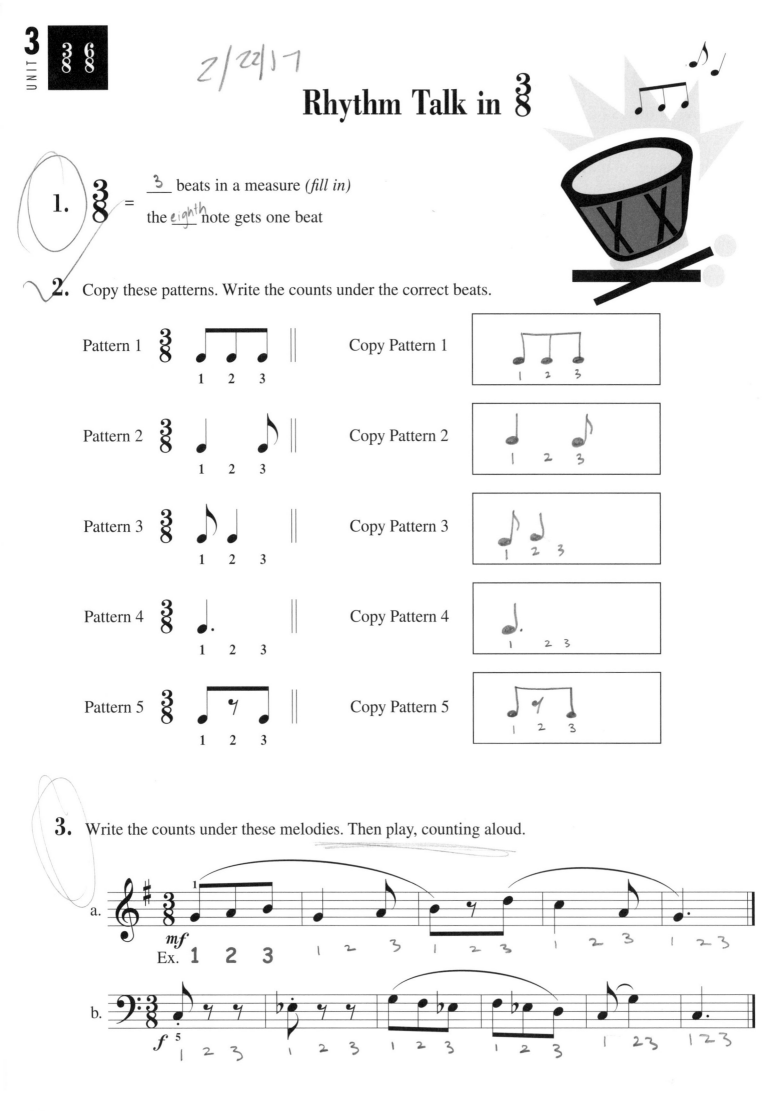

1. $\frac{3}{8}$ = __3__ beats in a measure *(fill in)*

the _eighth_ note gets one beat

2. Copy these patterns. Write the counts under the correct beats.

Pattern 1 — Copy Pattern 1

Pattern 2 — Copy Pattern 2

Pattern 3 — Copy Pattern 3

Pattern 4 — Copy Pattern 4

Pattern 5 — Copy Pattern 5

3. Write the counts under these melodies. Then play, counting aloud.

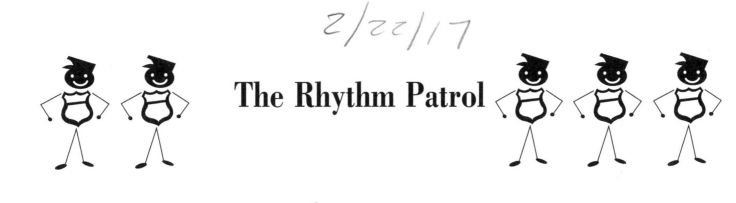

The Rhythm Patrol

The *Daily News* reported that mistakes in $\frac{3}{8}$ rhythm are at the highest number in 20 years.
Time to call The Rhythm Patrol!

4. Put an "X" through each *incorrect measure* for the $\frac{3}{8}$ rhythms below. Find all eight errors!

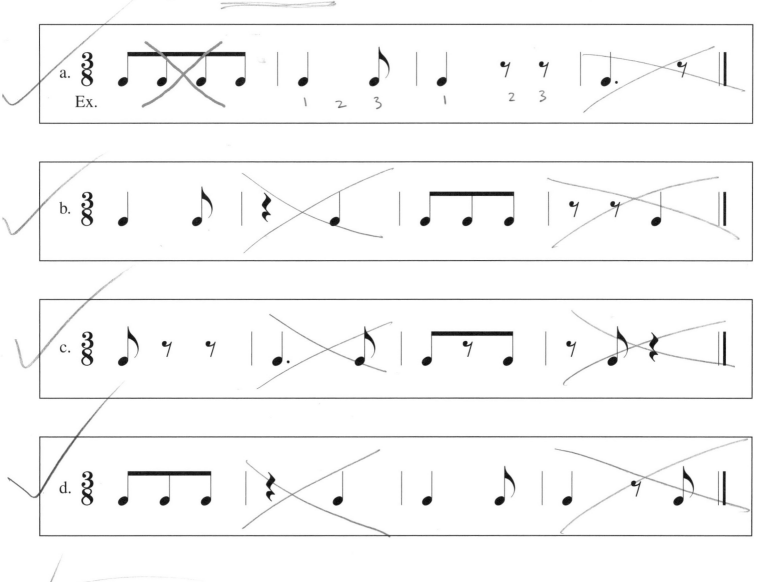

Your Own $\frac{3}{8}$ Rhythm

5. Now write four measures of your own rhythm. Think patterns! See Patterns 1–5 on page 14.
Then tap your rhythm.

(you write)

Lesson p.27 (Scarborough Fair)

Rhythm Talk in $\frac{6}{8}$

1. $\frac{6}{8}$ = <u>6</u> beats in a measure *(fill in)*

the <u>eighth</u> note gets one beat

2. Copy these patterns. Write the counts under the correct beats.

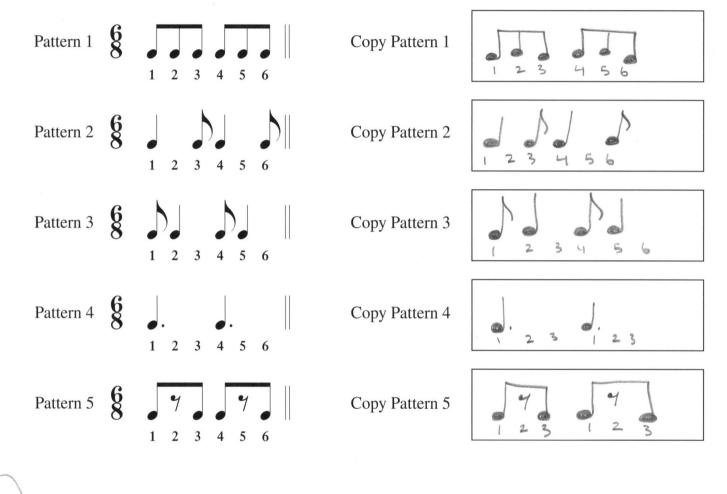

Pattern 1 $\frac{6}{8}$ 1 2 3 4 5 6   Copy Pattern 1   1 2 3 4 5 6

Pattern 2 $\frac{6}{8}$ 1 2 3 4 5 6   Copy Pattern 2   1 2 3 4 5 6

Pattern 3 $\frac{6}{8}$ 1 2 3 4 5 6   Copy Pattern 3   1 2 3 4 5 6

Pattern 4 $\frac{6}{8}$ 1 2 3 4 5 6   Copy Pattern 4   1 2 3 1 2 3

Pattern 5 $\frac{6}{8}$ 1 2 3 4 5 6   Copy Pattern 5   1 2 3 1 2 3

3. Write the correct time signature for each example: $\frac{2}{4}$ $\frac{3}{4}$ $\frac{4}{4}$ $\frac{3}{8}$ $\frac{6}{8}$

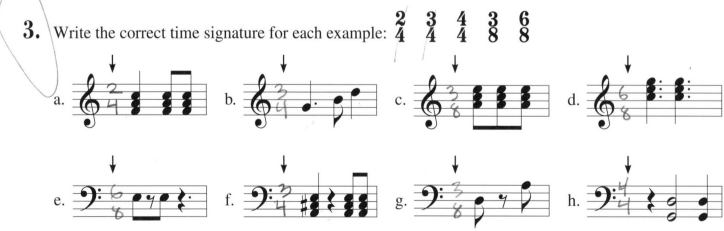

a.   b.   c.   d.

e.   f.   g.   h.

EYE TRAINING

Circle every set of ♩♪♪♩ in the music.
Feel **2 beats** per measure as you sightread.

sightread

a.

Count: 1   2   1   2   1   2   1   2

• Circle every set of ♩ ♪ in the music. Feel **2 beats** per measure as you sightread.

b.

Count: 1   2   1   2   1   2   1   2

• Write four measures of your own rhythms. Think $\frac{3}{8}+\frac{3}{8}$. Then tap your rhythm. (See page 16.)

$\frac{6}{8}$ | | | ‖

(you write)

EAR TRAINING

Your teacher will play either example **a** or **b**. Circle the example you hear.
Your teacher may ask you to play each rhythm on the piano.

1a.

or

b.

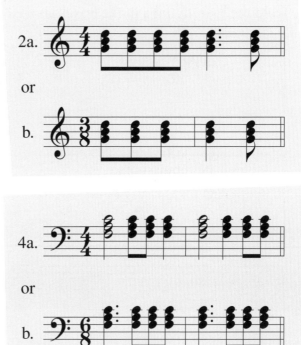

2a.

or

b.

3a.

or

b.

4a.

or

b.

The Triplet

4/19/17.

Sometimes **3 eighth notes** can be equal to a quarter note.

This is called a *triplet*.

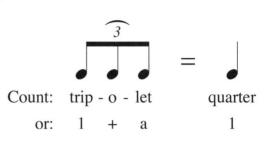

Count: trip - o - let   quarter

or: 1   +   a   1

1. Say these words aloud. Then draw a line to the rhythm on the right that matches the rhythm of the words.

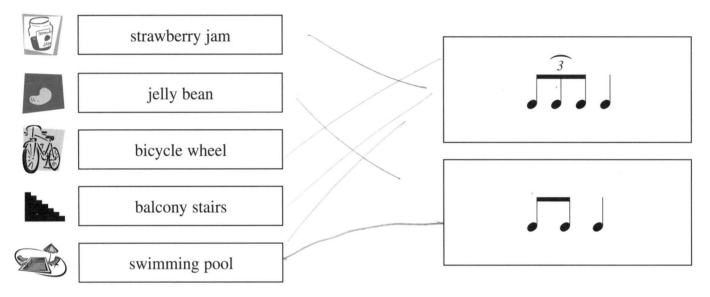

- strawberry jam
- jelly bean
- bicycle wheel
- balcony stairs
- swimming pool

2. In each box, write the rhythm that correctly matches the words given. Choose from the two rhythms in the boxes above.

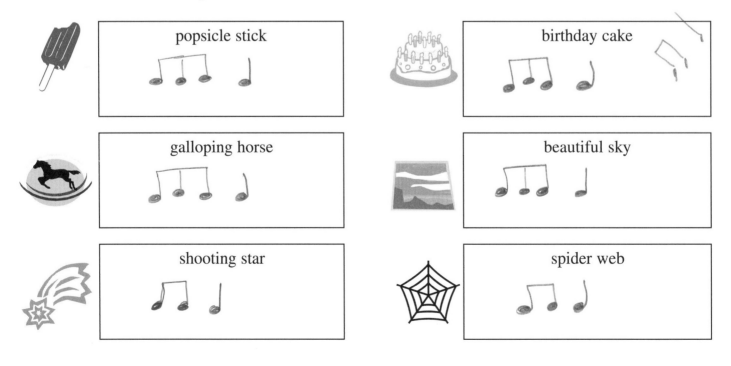

popsicle stick

birthday cake

galloping horse

beautiful sky

shooting star

spider web

Draw the Bar Lines!

1. Add bar lines after every **2 beats**. Then write "1-2" under the correct notes.

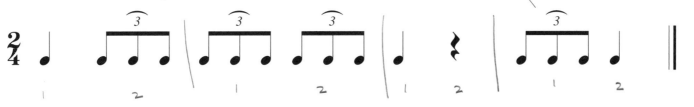

2. Add bar lines after every **3 beats**. Then write "1-2-3" under the correct notes.

3. Add bar lines after every **4 beats**. Then write "1-2-3-4" under the correct notes.

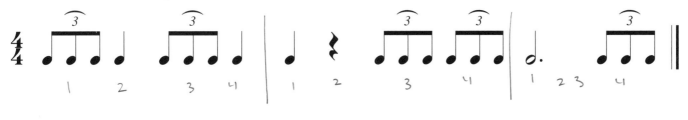

4. Tap each rhythm above for your teacher with the metronome ticking at ♩ = 84.

5. Put an X through each *incorrect* measure. It may have too many or too few beats.

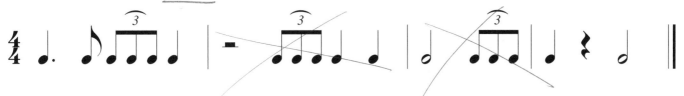

6. Choose a time signature: **2/4**, **3/4**, or **4/4** and write your own rhythm using triplets.

time
signature

Drummer at the Piano

4/26/17

1. • Draw **bar lines** for the three rhythms below. Notice each time signature.

• Tap each two-handed rhythm with your teacher.
Before you begin, count *one free measure* that subdivides each beat into triplets.

Count-off: **1** + a   **2** + a

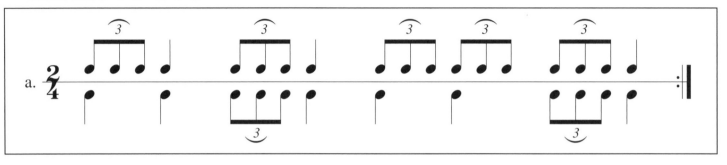

Count-off: **1** + a   **2** + a   **3** + a

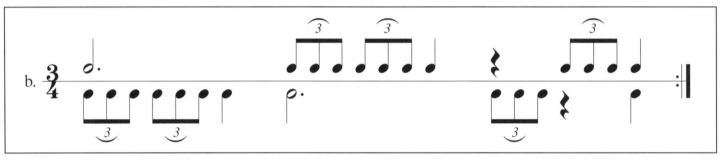

Count-off: **1** + a   **2** + a   **3** + a   **4** + a

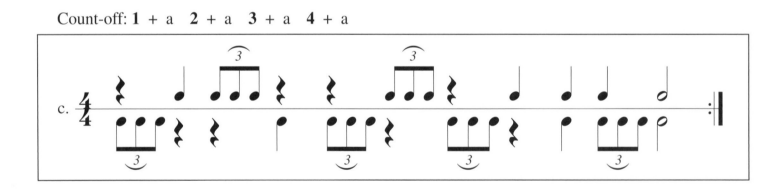

2.

Play the $\frac{2}{4}$ rhythm
on **D minor** chords.

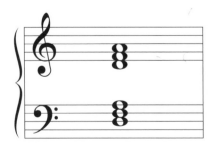

Play the $\frac{3}{4}$ rhythm
on **A minor** chords.

Play the $\frac{4}{4}$ rhythm
on **C minor** chords.

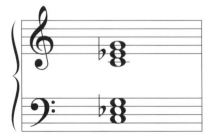

Triplet Tunes

The melodies below use **triplets**.
First notice each key signature and time signature.
Then set a slow, steady beat and sightread.

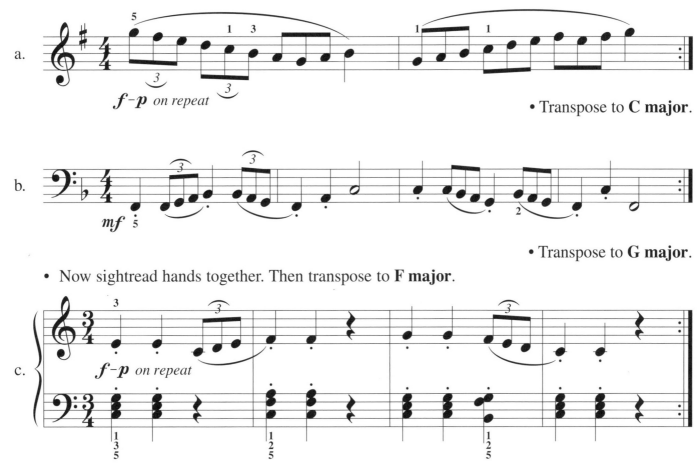

a.

f-*p* *on repeat*

• Transpose to **C major**.

b.

mf

• Transpose to **G major**.

• Now sightread hands together. Then transpose to **F major**.

c.

f-*p* *on repeat*

Your teacher will play a musical example.

Listen Well!

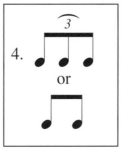

Do you hear 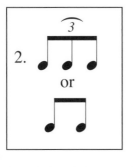 (triplets) or 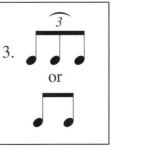 (two eighths)?
Circle the rhythm you hear.

1.   or

2.   or

3.   or

4.   or

For Teacher Use Only (The examples may be played in any order and repeated, if needed.)

f   *mp*

mf   *mf*

Lesson pp.36–37 (Amazing Grace)   21

Bass Ledger Notes

Ledger lines are used to extend the staff below low F.
Notes are written *on* the ledger lines and *in* the spaces.

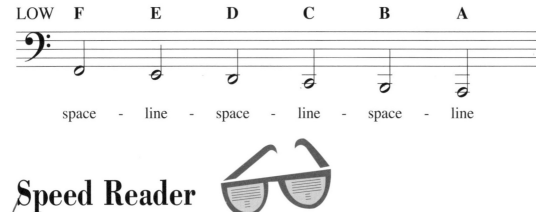

| LOW | F | E | D | C | B | A |

space - line - space - line - space - line

Speed Reader

1. • Cover the notes above and name the ledger notes below.
As you read ledger lines and spaces, it may be helpful to think in **3rds**.

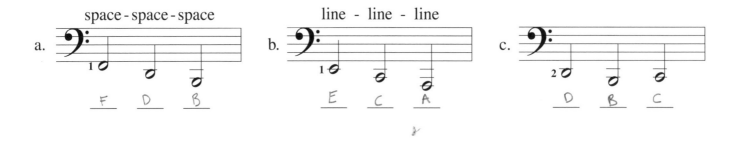

space - space - space

a. F D B

line - line - line

b. E C A

c. D B C

• Try four notes!

d. F D E C

e. C A B E

f. D F E C

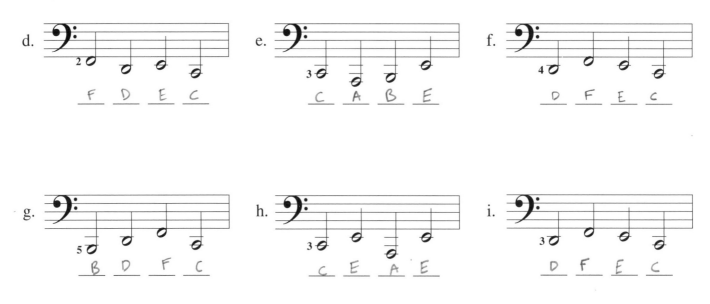

g. B D F C

h. C E A E

i. D F E C

• Your teacher may ask you to play each example on the piano.

Name the Interval

5/17/17

2. Name the interval played by the string bass:
2nd   3rd   4th   5th   6th   7th   8ve

a. _5th_

b. _3rd_

c. _4th_ 2nd

d.

e. _3rd_

f. _7th_

g. _8ve_

h. _5th_

i. _3rd_ 2nd

j. _7th_ 6th

k. _5th_ 3rd

l. _7th_

Spell the Word

3. Spell these words using **bass ledger lines**. Use whole notes.

C   A   B   Ex.

F   E   E   D

D   A   B

F   A   D   E

B   A   D   G   E

B   E   A   D

Treble Ledger Notes

Ledger lines are used to extend the staff above high G.
Remember, notes are written *on* the ledger lines and *in* the spaces.

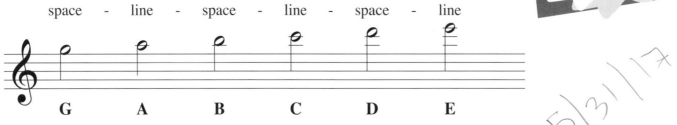

space - line - space - line - space - line

G   A   B   C   D   E

5/31/17

In the Clouds!

1. • Cover the note names above. Then write the **note names** and the interval in the blanks below.

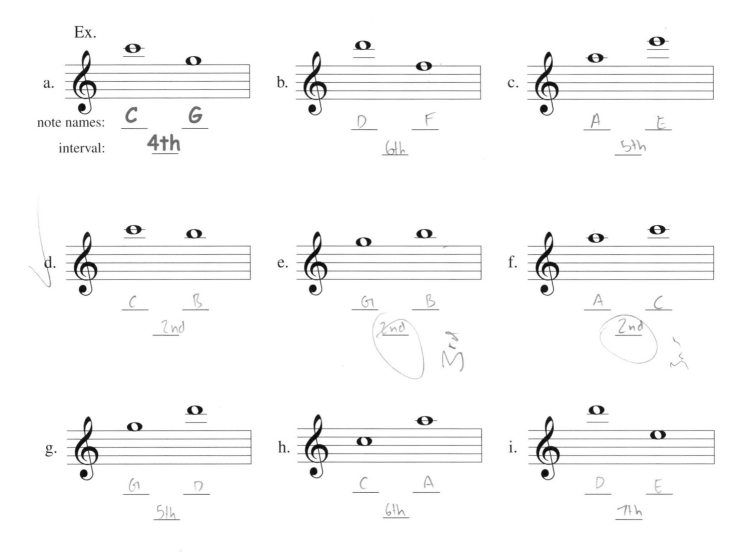

Ex.

a. note names: C   G
interval: **4th**

b. D   F
6th

c. A   E
5th

d. C   B
2nd

e. G   B
2nd   3rd

f. A   C
2nd

g. G   D
5th

h. C   A
6th

i. D   E
7th

• Your teacher may ask you to play the examples above on the piano.

Target Practice

2. • Draw a line connecting each note on the staff to the correct key on the keyboard.

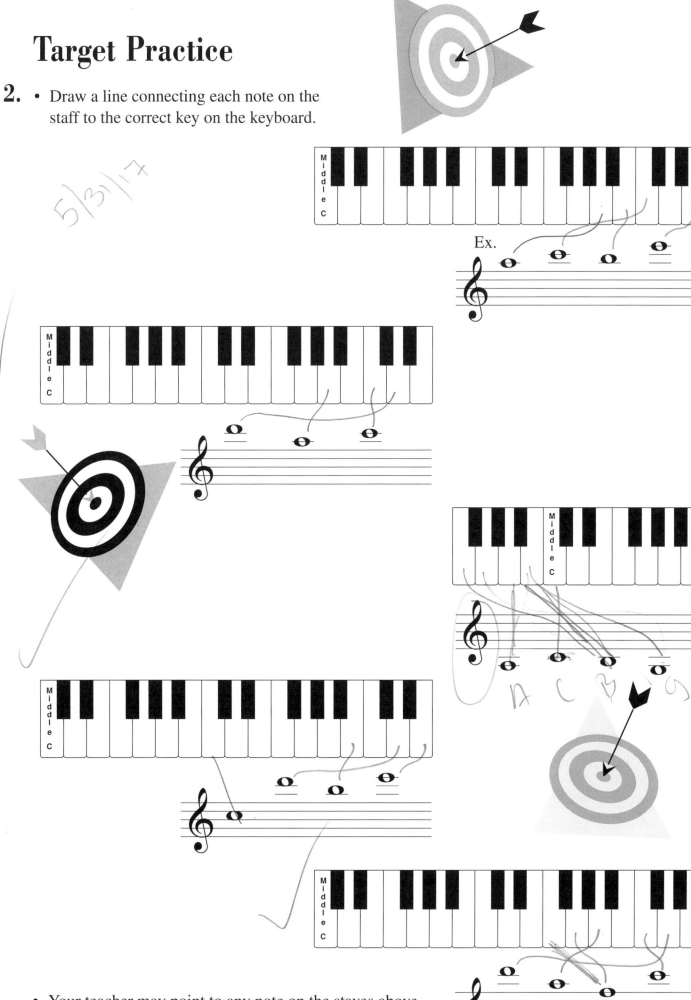

• Your teacher may point to any note on the staves above. See how quickly you can play it on the keyboard!

Lesson pp.44–45 (The Great Wall of China)   25

First notice each *key signature* and *time signature*.
Then set a slow, steady beat and sightread.

Ledger Tunes

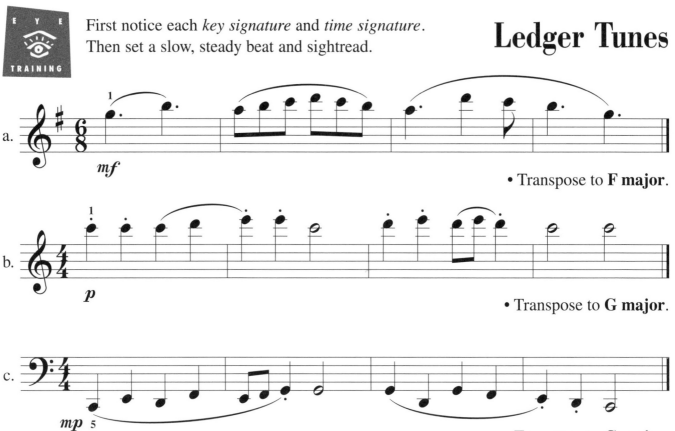

a. *mf*

• Transpose to **F major**.

b. *p*

• Transpose to **G major**.

c. *mp*

• Transpose to **G major**.

Mystery Notes

Your teacher will play the two notes given, and then a "mystery note."*
It will be a **2nd or a 3rd higher or lower** from the *last* note given.
Listen carefully and write the "mystery note" you hear.

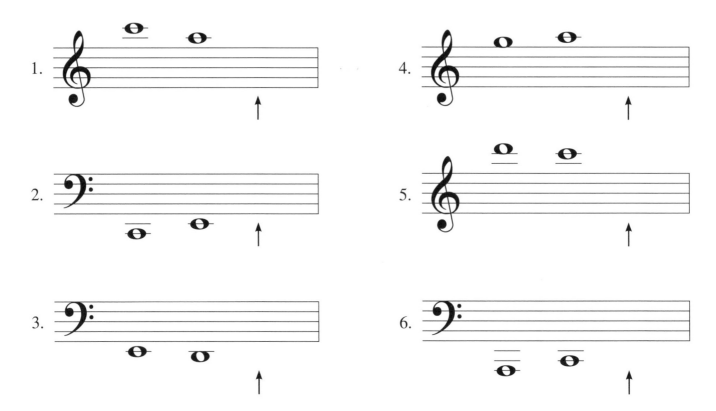

*Teacher Note: Play the example and add a note a 2nd or 3rd higher or lower.
Check the student's answer after each example is played.

Chord Guy's Music Test

(Review of UNITS 1–5)

6/14

1. a. A 7th is from *a line to a line* or *a space to a space*. (**True** or False) (circle)

b. Draw a 7th up or down from each note. Then name both notes.

↑ a 7th   ↓ a 7th   ↑ a 7th

Note
names: G   F   A   G   D   C

2. a. In $\frac{3}{8}$ time, a ♩ = 1 beat.   True or (**False**)

b. Write a $\frac{3}{8}$ or $\frac{3}{4}$ time signature for the examples below.

$\frac{3}{8}$ $\frac{3}{4}$

3. a. In a fast tempo, $\frac{6}{8}$ time can be felt with 2 beats per measure. (**True** or False)
What note receives the beat?   ♪   or   ♩   or   (♩.)   (circle)

b. Complete the measures below using these rhythms: ♫♪,   ♩♪,   or   ♩.

$\frac{6}{8}$

you write   *you write*   *you write*

4. a. A triplet means $\frac{3}{4}$ time.   True or (**False**)

b. Using only triplets ♩♩♩, complete the measures below.

$\frac{4}{4}$

7/12/17

Write the Chromatic Scale

A **chromatic scale** has 12 tones and uses only half steps.

1. • Name the notes of the *ascending* chromatic scale. Notice as the scale goes up, **sharps** are used.

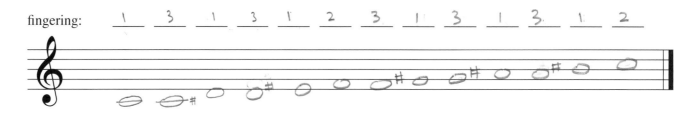

note names: C C# D D# E F F# G G# A A# B C

• Copy the ascending chromatic scale above. Remember to use sharps!
• Write the R.H. fingering in the blanks below. You may check yourself at the piano.

fingering: 1 3 1 3 1 2 3 1 3 1 3 1 2

2. • Name the notes of the *descending* chromatic scale. Notice as the scale goes down, **flats** are used.

note names: C B Bb A Ab G Gb F E Eb D Db C

• Copy the descending chromatic scale above. Remember to use flats!
• Write the L.H. fingering in the blanks below. You may check yourself at the piano.

fingering: 1 2 3 1 3 1 3 1 2 1 3 1 3

—Check fingering   3 1 3 1

3. • Close your eyes and picture the keyboard!
   • Name aloud the notes of the chromatic scale from C **up** to C.
   • Name aloud the notes of the chromatic scale from C **down** to C.

The Composer's Laboratory

Composers use a variety of sounds in their music.

The **chromatic** scale, **major** scale, and **whole tone** scale (made up of all whole steps) are some of the tools a composer can use.

1. Circle the correct label for each scale in the following examples.

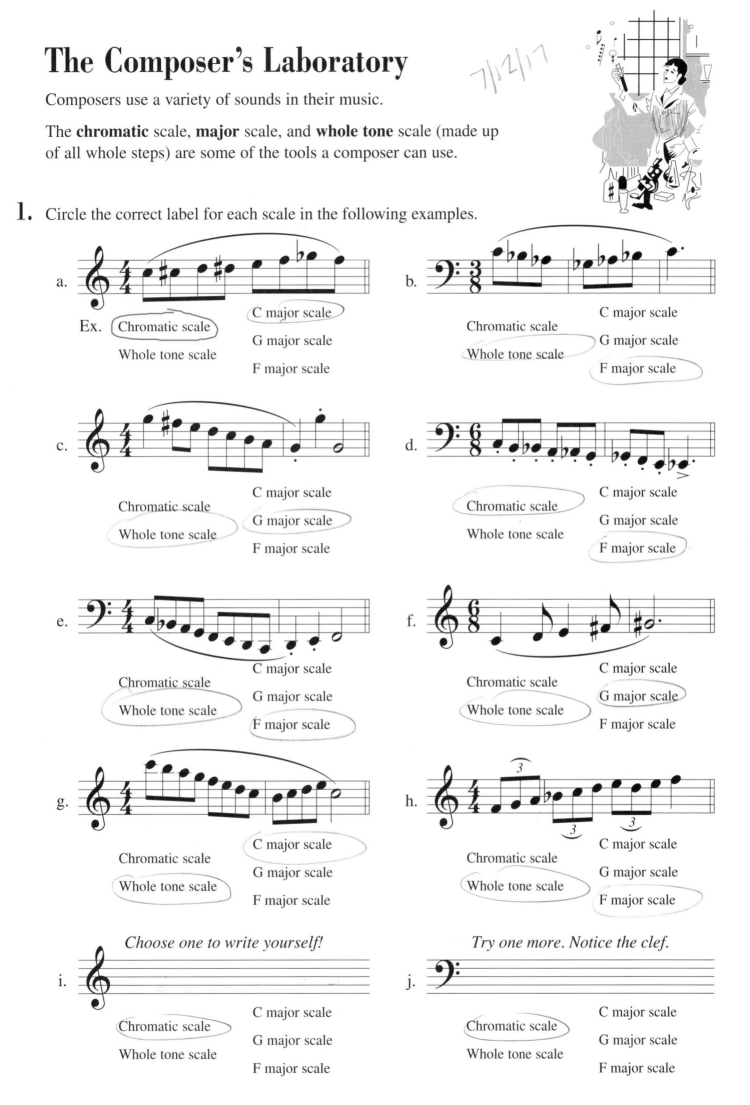

a.
Ex. (Chromatic scale)
Whole tone scale
(C major scale)
G major scale
F major scale

b.
Chromatic scale
(Whole tone scale)
C major scale
G major scale
(F major scale)

c.
Chromatic scale
(Whole tone scale)
C major scale
(G major scale)
F major scale

d.
(Chromatic scale)
Whole tone scale
C major scale
G major scale
(F major scale)

e.
Chromatic scale
(Whole tone scale)
C major scale
G major scale
(F major scale)

f.
Chromatic scale
(Whole tone scale)
C major scale
(G major scale)
F major scale

g.
Chromatic scale
(Whole tone scale)
(C major scale)
G major scale
F major scale

h.
Chromatic scale
(Whole tone scale)
C major scale
G major scale
(F major scale)

Choose one to write yourself!

i.
(Chromatic scale)
Whole tone scale
C major scale
G major scale
F major scale

Try one more. Notice the clef.

j.
(Chromatic scale)
Whole tone scale
C major scale
G major scale
F major scale

2. Circle three examples that use the chromatic scale. Think *half steps!*

Music for a Time Machine

Chromatic Scale Improvisation

3. Improvise music for a time machine!

- First, listen to your teacher play the accompaniment.

- Then with your R.H., play a few notes from the **chromatic scale** IN ANY ORDER. Start with a very L-O-N-G note, then another L-O-N-G note. Gradually let your fingers experiment with other notes using any note values.

- Your teacher will tell you, "Bring the time machine back to the present." Play any C and hold.

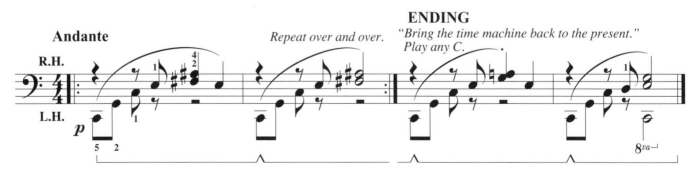

Teacher Improv Accompaniment (Student improvises higher on the keyboard.)

Look for Half Steps!

Circle the **half step** in each example below.

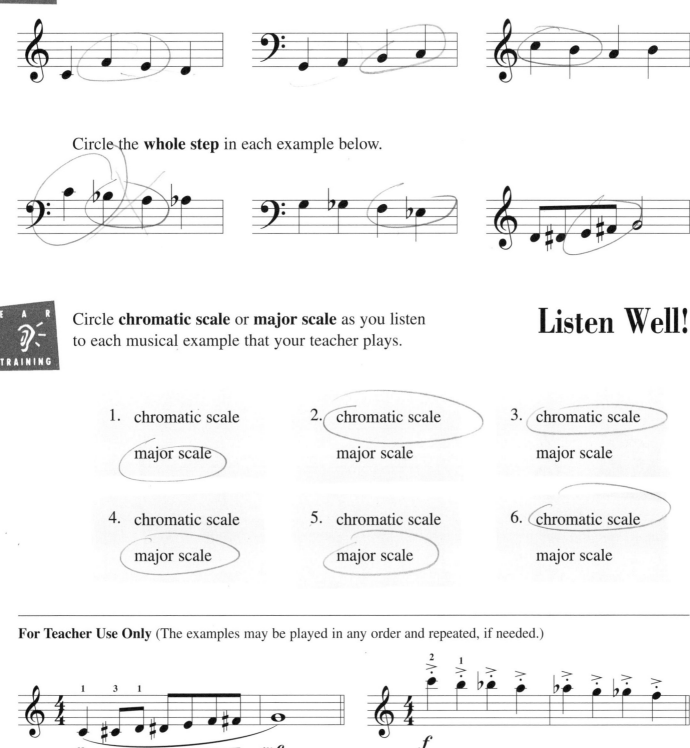

Circle the **whole step** in each example below.

Circle **chromatic scale** or **major scale** as you listen
to each musical example that your teacher plays.

Listen Well!

1. chromatic scale

   major scale

2. *chromatic scale*

   major scale

3. *chromatic scale*

   major scale

4. chromatic scale

   major scale

5. chromatic scale

   major scale

6. *chromatic scale*

   major scale

For Teacher Use Only (The examples may be played in any order and repeated, if needed.)

7-5-17

Write the D Major Scale

1. The D major scale has 7 tones created from ___half___ steps and ___whole___ steps. *(fill in)*
The **half steps** occur between degrees ___1st___ and ___5th___ and degrees ___7th___ and ___1st___ .
All the other intervals are ___whole___ steps.

2. Trace, then copy the **D major key signature** three times. Name the two sharps.

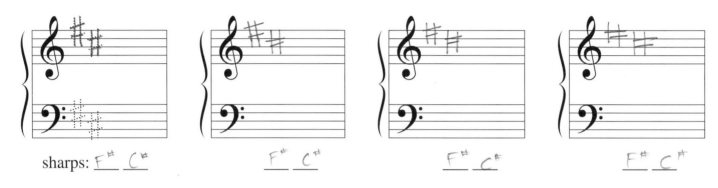

sharps: ___F#___ ___C#___   ___F#___ ___C#___   ___F#___ ___C#___   ___F#___ ___C#___

3. • Write the D major scale for each clef. Draw **sharps** in front of the correct notes.
 • Number the scale degrees 1–8.
 • Use a ⌐⌐ to mark the *whole steps*. Use a ∨ to mark the *half steps*. (See page 2 for review.)

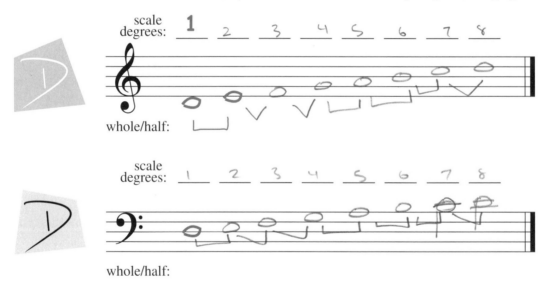

4. Label each note as **tonic** (scale degree 1), **dominant** (degree 5), or **leading tone** (degree 7).

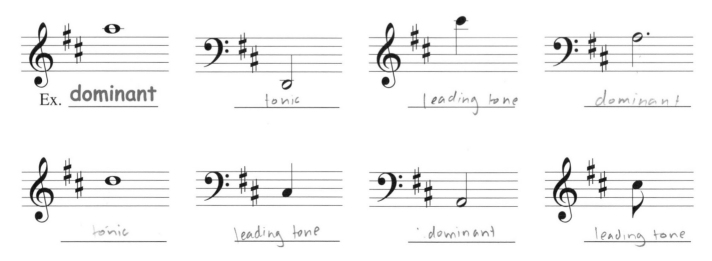

Ex. **dominant**   ___tonic___   ___leading tone___   ___dominant___

___tonic___   ___leading tone___   ___dominant___   ___leading tone___

7-5-17

Harmonize in D Major: I, IV, V7 Chords

5. Copy each chord and its Roman numeral.

5#: 235 **I**   I

(you write)

146 **IV** IV

2457 **V7** V7

6. • First play the R.H. melody.

• Then harmonize it with **I**, **IV**, or **V7** chords.
Play with blocked chords.

Street Dance

Moderato

Ex. **I**   IV   V7 IV V7   I   V7   I

5   I   V7   V7   I

9   I   IV   V7 I V7   I   V7   I

"Canoe Ride" Improvisation

7. *Listen* to the teacher accompaniment. When ready, improvise a melody
using notes from the D major scale **in any order**. Remember the **F♯** and **C♯**!

• Play D major blocked and broken chords.
• Play repeated notes, especially on the *tonic* (D) and *dominant* (A).
• Make up short musical patterns. Repeat them *forte* and then *piano*.

Teacher Duet: (Student improvises higher using the D major scale.)

R.H.

L.H.   *mf - pp*   *mp*

Lesson pp.54–55 (Simple Gifts)

First name aloud each L.H. chord (**I**, **IV**, or **V7**).
Then sightread this music in D major.

Strolling Along

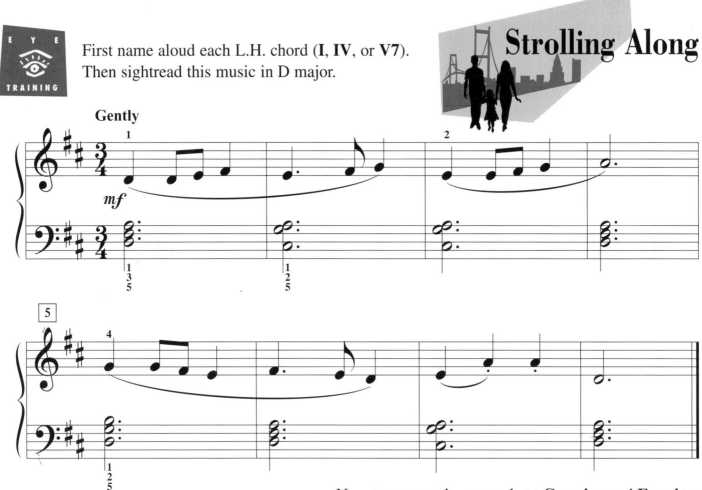

Gently

• Now transpose the example to **G major** and **F major**.

Your teacher will play a chord pattern in the
Key of D. Circle the chord pattern you hear.
The teacher plays **a** or **b** using these chords.

Listen for Chords

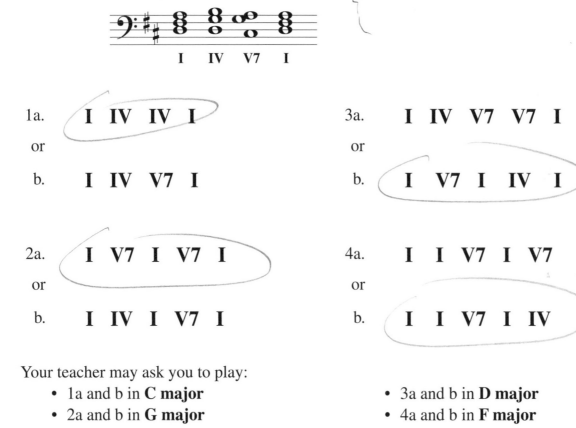

I   IV   V7   I

1a.   I IV IV I

or

b.   I IV V7 I

2a.   I V7 I V7 I

or

b.   I IV I V7 I

3a.   I IV V7 V7 I

or

b.   I V7 I IV I

4a.   I I V7 I V7

or

b.   I I V7 I IV

Your teacher may ask you to play:

• 1a and b in **C major**
• 2a and b in **G major**

• 3a and b in **D major**
• 4a and b in **F major**

Major and Minor Chord Chart

(Review of UNITS 1–7)

8/2/17

- Complete the chart for each chord by **naming** the keys, **identifying** the chord, and **notating** it on the staff.

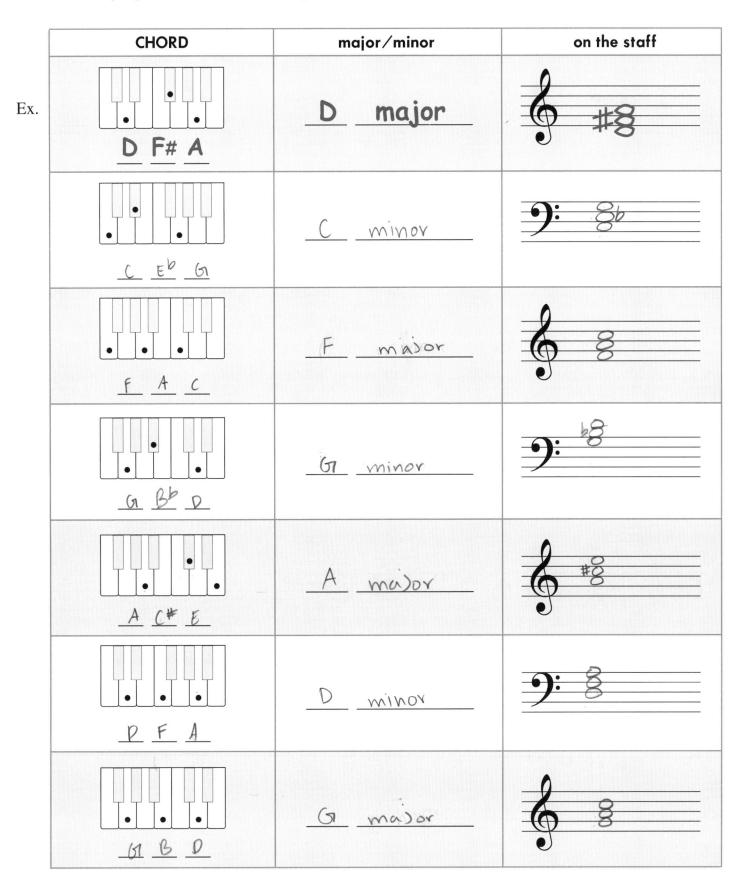

CHORD	major/minor	on the staff
Ex. D F# A	D major	#8
C E♭ G	C minor	8♭
F A C	F major	8
G B♭ D	G minor	♭8
A C# E	A major	#8
D F A	D minor	8
G B D	G major	8

The One-Octave Arpeggio

An *arpeggio* uses **chord tones** played up or down the keyboard.
Remember, for a one-octave arpeggio, the hand is extended over the keys.

Ex. **C major chord tones** (C - E - G - C)
Notice four tones are shaded.

Ex. **C major one-octave arpeggio**

fingering: 1 2 3 5 3 2 1

1. • Fill in the **D minor chord tones** below.
(There are 4.)

• Write the D minor arpeggio and fingering below.

fingering: 1 2 3 5 3 2 1

2. • Fill in the **E minor chord tones** below.

• Write the E minor arpeggio and fingering below.

fingering: 1 2 3 5 3 2 1

3. • Fill in the **G major chord tones** below.
Notice the clef!

• Write the G major arpeggio and fingering below.

fingering: 5 4 2 1 2 4 5

4. • Fill in the **A minor chord tones** below.

• Write the A minor arpeggio and fingering below.

fingering: 5 4 2 1 2 4 5

• Your teacher may ask you to play each arpeggio you have written.

Magic Fingering

- Write the correct fingering for each example below.
  You may check yourself by playing them on the piano.

C major arpeggio

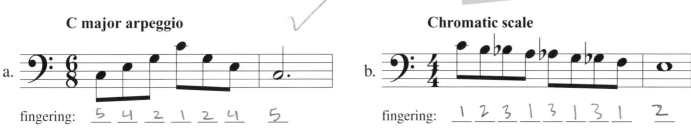

a.

fingering: 5 4 2 1 2 4 5

Chromatic scale

b.

fingering: 1 2 3 1 3 1 3 1 2

F major scale

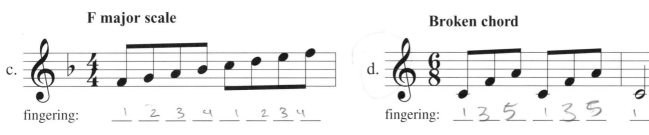

c.

fingering: 1 2 3 4 1 2 3 4

Broken chord

d.

fingering: 1 3 5 1 3 5 1

D major arpeggio

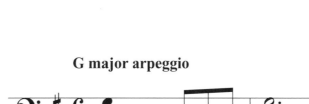

e.

fingering: 1 2 3 5 3 2 1

G major arpeggio

f.

fingering: 1 2 4 5 4 2 1

Alberti bass

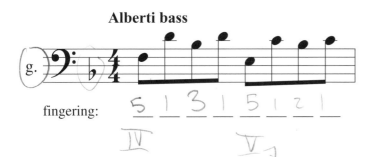

g.

fingering: 5 1 3 1 5 1 2 1

IV   V₇

A minor arpeggio

h.

fingering: 5 2 3 1 2 3 5

G major scale

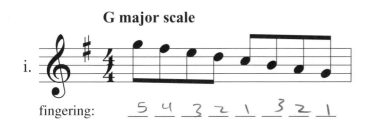

i.

fingering: 5 4 3 2 1 3 2 1

Chromatic scale

j.

fingering: 1 2 3 1 3 1 3 1 2

You Can Compose!

1. Complete this piece by composing your own melody over the L.H. one-octave arpeggios.

Follow these steps:

a. Play the L.H. alone. Take note of the boxed chord symbols that indicate the harmony.

b. Use the suggested rhythm for your melody shown above the staff. Think **chord tones**! These will blend well with the harmony.

c. Experiment and feel free to change a melody note even after you have written it down.

8/23/17

2. Play and enjoy your composition!

Nighttime Novela

by _____Sona_____

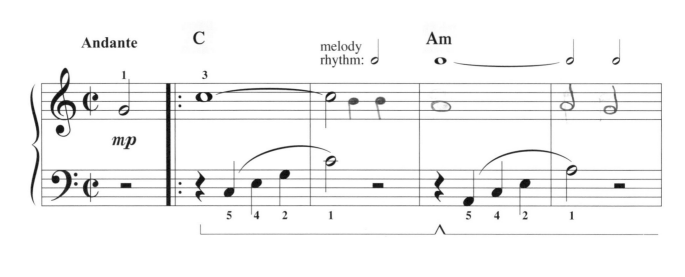

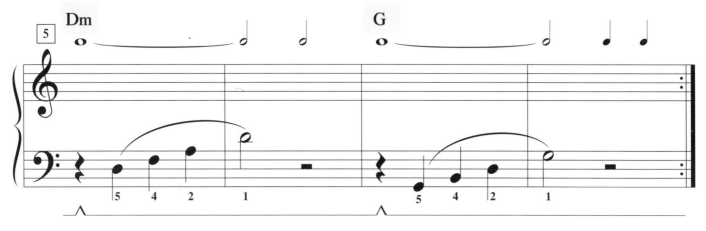

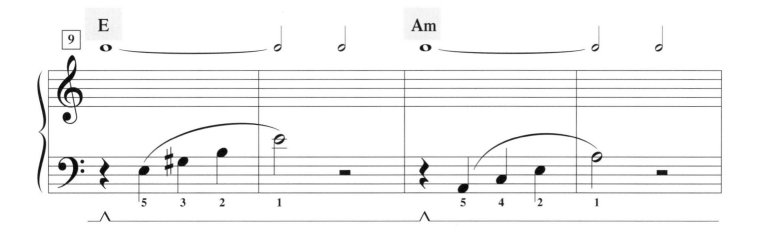

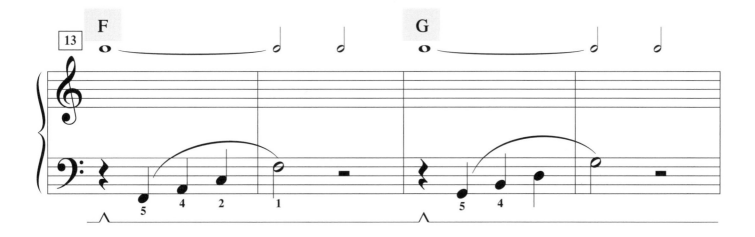

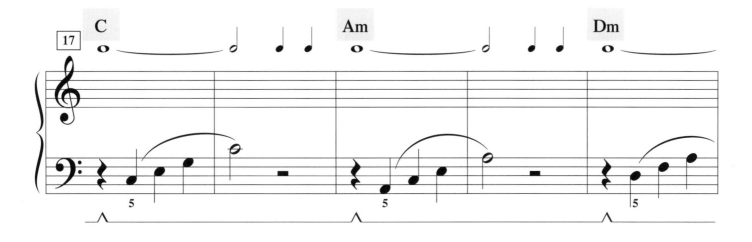

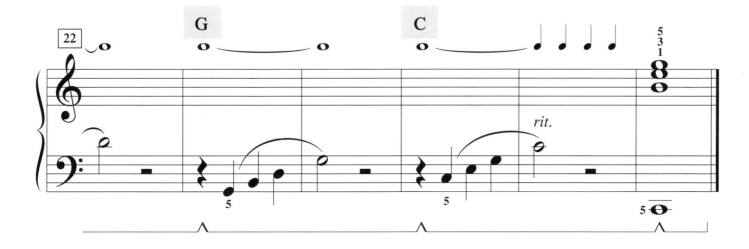

Final Review (UNITS 1-8)

8/23/17

- Complete each musical example.

2. Name the intervals.

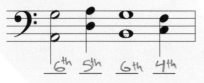

6th 5th 6th 4th

4. Write four measures of $\frac{3}{8}$ rhythm.
Make each measure different.

6. Name these ledger notes.

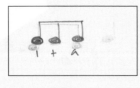

A E D B C

8. *ff* means ___fortissimo___.

10. Draw a triplet and write
the counts (1 + a).

13. Write the letter names of the D scale. Include sharps.

D E F# G A B C# D

15. Write three measures of $\frac{6}{8}$ rhythm.
Make each measure different.

1. **A B** form is also known as
___binary form___.

|: **A** :|: **B** :|

3. **A B A** form is also called
___Ternary form___.

5. Name the key signatures.

G

D

F

7. Playing 8th notes in a
long-short pattern is called
___swing___ rhythm.

9. ¢ means __4__ beats per measure.

11. Name the scale that
only uses half steps.
___chromatic scale___

12. Write the beats "1 2" under the correct notes.

¢ 1 2 3 4 | 1 + 2 + 3 4 | 1 2 3 4 |

14. Name these notes.

A E D B C

Congratulations!
You have completed the book!